Visions of
LONDON

Simon Hadleigh-Sparks

Visions of
LONDON

Simon Hadleigh-Sparks

Southwark Underground

INTRODUCTION

Visions of London is a collection of urban city photography by award-winning photographer Simon Hadleigh-Sparks. The book highlights his passion for abstract-reflected architecture and reflected imagery, a style he has created for himself. He also experiments with extreme contrasts and has been called "a master of light". He has also mastered the art of post-production – blending, temperature, tone curve, and luminance, just to mention just a few.

Simon has been described as 'a digital artist' as a major aspect of his urban photography is his ability to open up a new perspective on the city – its spaces, people and history by abstract photography and innovative digital techniques to reimagine and transform the structures that make up the London Skyline.

Buildings are twisted and contorted, landscapes manipulated, all to create a dynamic new look that will change the way you see one of the greatest cities in the world. Put simply, Simon views the world differently – everything has the potential to be a photographic moment. When out photographing on the street, he often remembers to look up. His eye for clean lines, architectural design and subtle incorporation of human elements give his images a uniqueness that stays true to his fascinating style.

Simon has been the recipient of multiple international awards and recent successes include winner and best in show at the 2014 London Photo Festival, highly commended in the 2014 Urban Photographer of the Year, and 3rd place in the monochrome category of the 2014 International Garden Photographer of the Year Awards. He also had various works exhibited in 2013/2014 in and around London. His photos can currently be seen on a number of websites, blogs and magazine articles.

Simon Hadleigh-Sparks is also a professional gardener in Syon Park, West London, a husband and a father. His photography is a passion; he goes from strength to strength, sharing his photos and maybe inspiring some people along the way. He has a mixture of styles and it is in post-production that Simon produces his most successful photography. This is his second book for New Holland Publishers, following Iconic London (2015).

Greenwich O2 Arena (The Millenium Dome)

Green Route – Embankment Underground

Shades Of Grey — Holborn

In The Middle — Willis Building

Royal Albert Hall London – 1871 to Now

You Wait Your Whole Life For A Single Moment Then Suddenly It's Today — Holborn

There Are Days Like This In London City

Cold & Warm – King's Cross Walkway

Eternally Reflected – Canary Wharf

16

Eye Candy – Paddington Basin

17

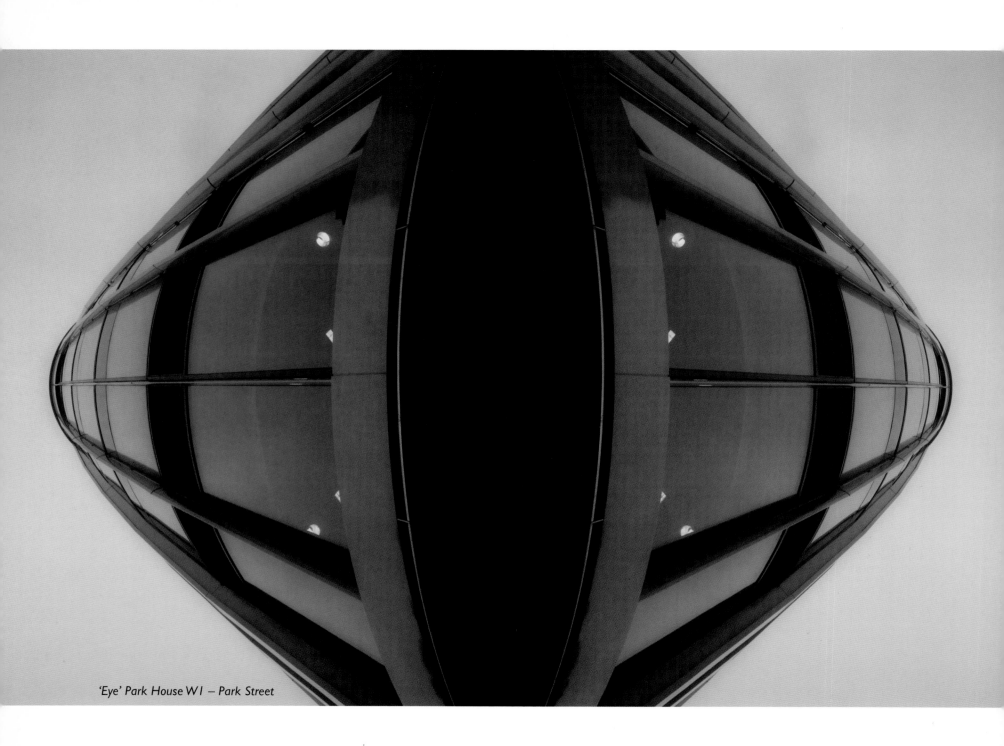

'Eye' Park House W1 – Park Street

Face Off 2 – Old Broad Street

Hive Mind – Office Building Cannon Street

Inside St Georges Wharf

I Wandered Lonely As A Cloud – Tower 42

I Don't Like Mondays – The Blue Fin Building

London Bridge 3D

London Bridge Underground

London's Big Wheel – London Eye

Martian Space Station – Albion Riverside Building

Noticed Impatience – Walkie Talkie

Construction – Provost Street

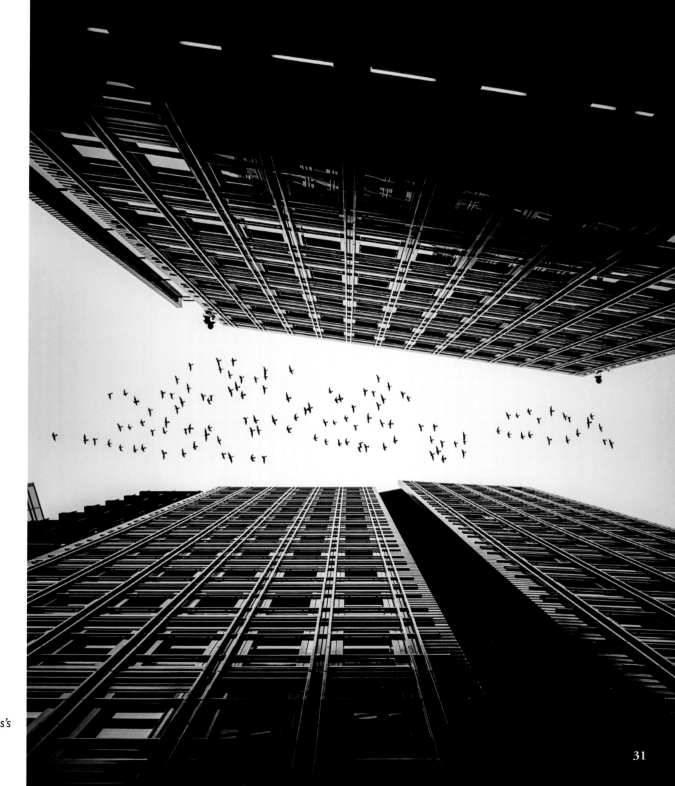

Flying South for Winter – St Giles's

Office Filing – Blackfriars Road

Skyscraper City Base Jumper – Canary Wharf

33

This Side of Paradise – Cheapside

Tholian Web – Canary Wharf

Tomorrow Is Yesterday – Broadgate

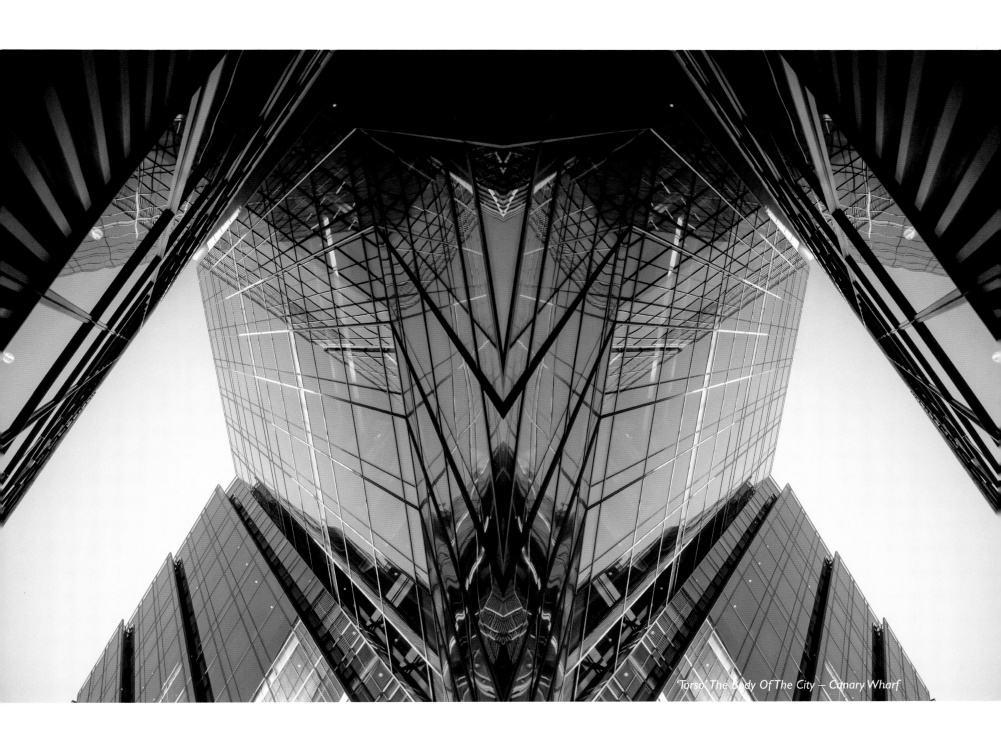

'Torso' The Body Of The City – Canary Wharf

Transformation Desire – The Borough

Trapped Inside – Blackfriars Road

Turning Upside – King's Cross Walkway

UFO London City Architecture –
Albion Building

Under The Bridge – Blackfriars Bridge

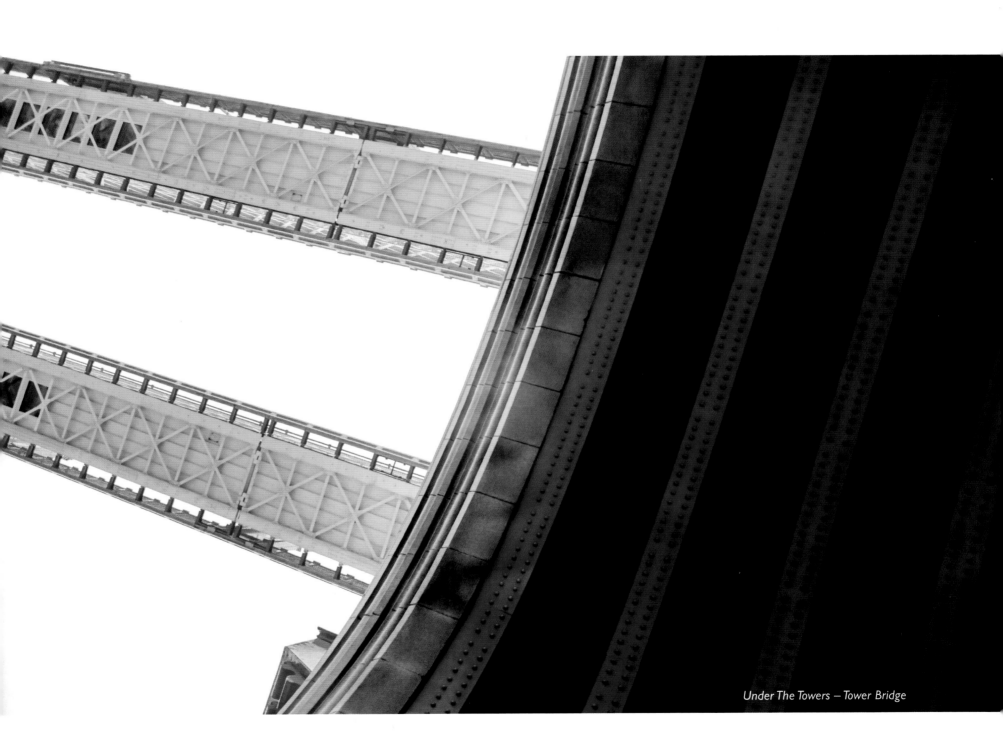

Under The Towers – Tower Bridge

Up & Over The Edge – North Row W1 Building

44

Urban City Love – City Point Tower Moorgate

Urban Erotica — Bishopsgate,
Bishops Square

Urban Flower – Seed Of The City – Lambeth Bridge

Vertical Skew – Willis Building

48

Vertigo 'Alien' – Office Life
London City – Blackfriars Road

49

Vertigo 'Harmony' – St Giles's

Where No One Has Gone Before – Walkie Talkie

Wink Of An Eye – Fitzrovia

Under Citypoint Skyscraper – Ropemaker Street

St Paul's Cathedral – Reflection Quadrilogy

All Our Yesterdays – London City Life – Buckingham Gate

Boris Bikes

Hadron Collider London Underground

Insane Geometry – Heron Quays

Southwark Underground Tube

Spliting The Atom - London City Underground

Ascent – Cheapside

Black Hole – Shoreditch

Blade Runner – Paddington Basin

Buildings Are Beauty – Paddington Basin

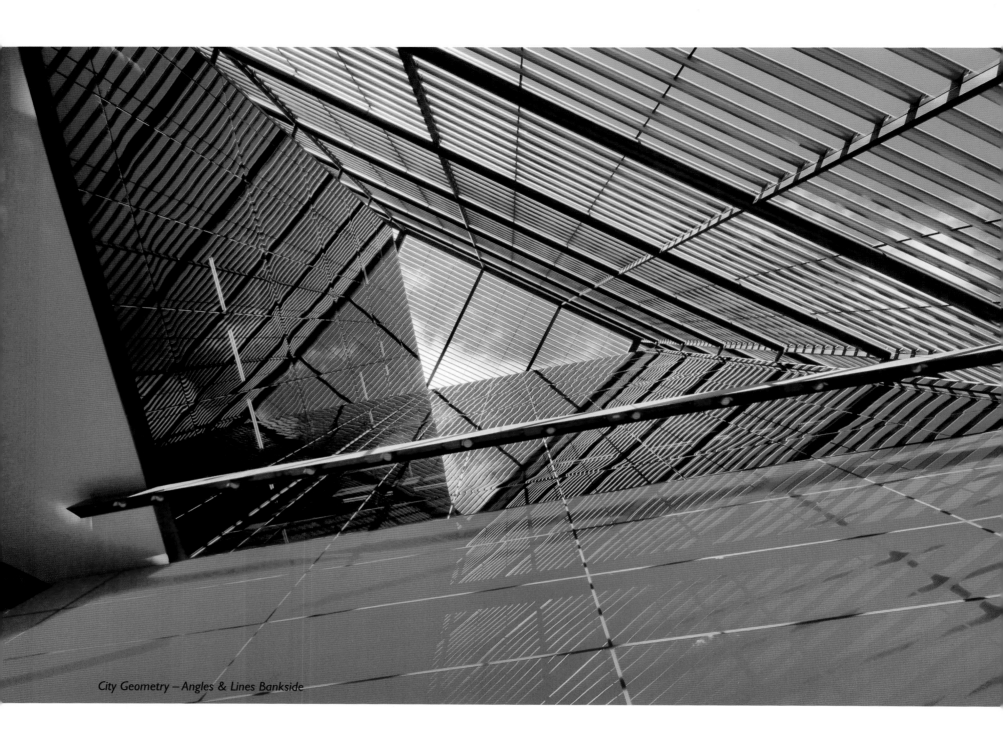

City Geometry – Angles & Lines Bankside

City Heat – Butler Place Westminster

Dimensional – The Borough

Do The Things You Want, Which You Only
Can Now — Sunset Rainbow — Bishopsgate

Don't Look Up – Castelnau

Elemental Signals – Bankside

Event Horizon – Park Plaza Hotel

Face Off – Bishopsgate

Face Your Demons – Southwark

Fantasy — London Wall

Freedom – London City Office Life – Aldgate

More Freedom – London City Office Life – Waterloo

Friday's Child – Bishopsgate

Going Up London – Willis Building

Golden Morning – Bankside

Good Morning London – Bishopsgate

I Once Towered Over London Before The Shard —
One Canada Square Canary Wharf

Is It Love or Obsession – London City

Is There In Truth No Beauty – Somers Town

Left My Heart In London – Tower Hill

Breakthrough — London Wall

Living In A Box – Broadgate

Around Every Corner – Bishopsgate

Only You Can Make Me Feel This Way –
Syon Park The Great Conservatory

Spiral Staircase – The Chapel of the Old Royal Naval College

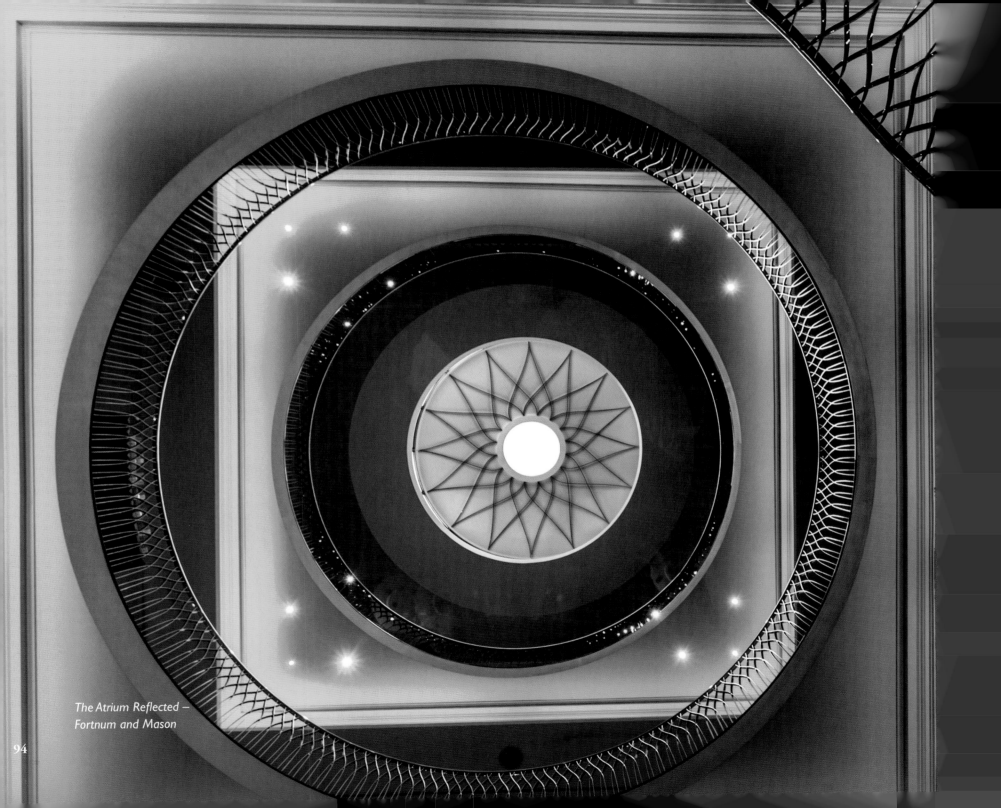

The Atrium Reflected –
Fortnum and Mason

94

*Where Does The Real World
Start - More London*

Aiming At Heaven — London BT Tower

Between The Looking Glass –
Lloyds Building & Willis Building

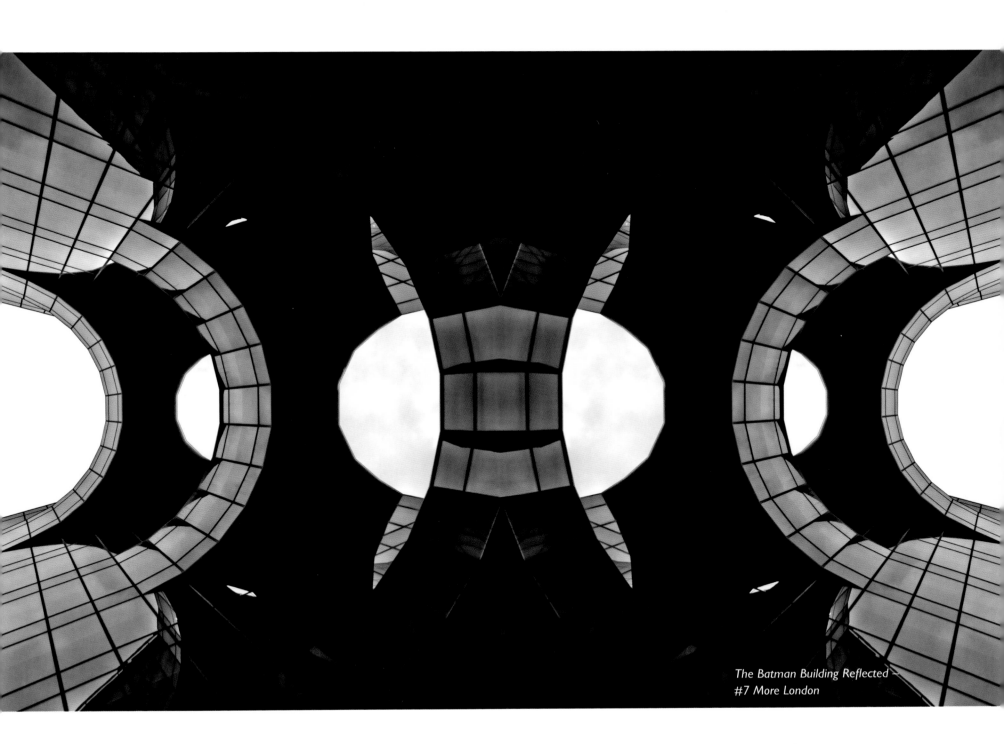

The Batman Building Reflected ~
#7 More London

London City Modern Architecture — Willis Building

Another Bond Street Underground

Bermondsey Underground London

Bermondsey Underground London

Bond Street Underground

London City Hall

City Hall & The Tower

Cubism London or London Tetris (New Version)

Palestra Building Blackfriars Road

Embankment Underground

Park Plaza Hotel – Westminster Bridge Road

Reflected Iconic Beauty — St Paul's Cathedral

London City Rocks – Fretboard In The Sky – West India Quay

There Are Days Like This In London City

115

*London Urban Life Goes Posh aka London Corset –
Paddington Basin*

Lonely World – Cheapside

Logan's Run – Westminster Underground

Matrix 3D – Monument Bankside

119

Matrix 4D – Monument Bankside

Metamorphosis – Bankside

Odd Future – Blackfriars Road

Office Lines – London Wall

Open Window – Canary Wharf

Perfect Days – The Borough

Phantom Of The Truth – London City Symmetry

Pipes & Lights – Lloyds Building

Reflected In Time — Southwark

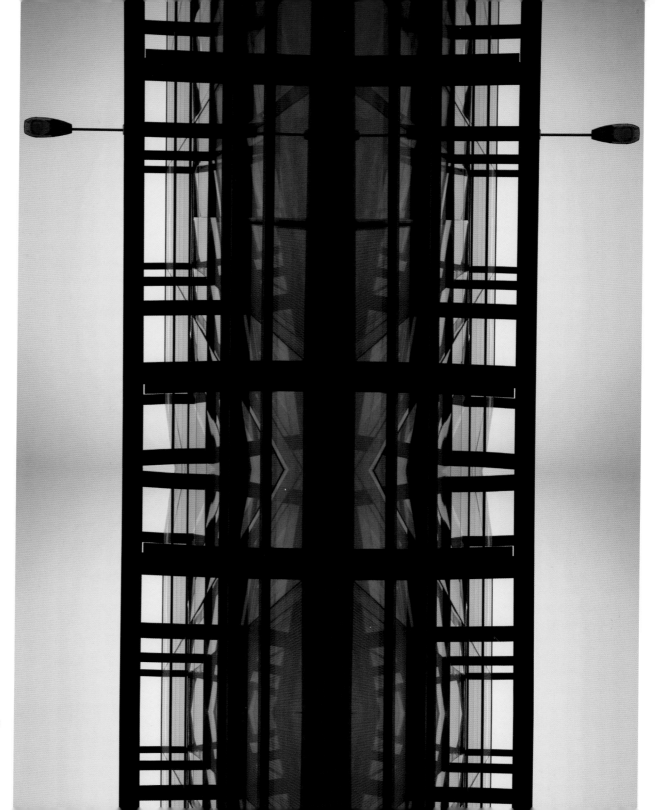

Reflected Symmetry Cheapside

Shout To The Top – Bankside

Sky Box – Marble Arch

Skyrise – From Black To White – Tower Hill

Sloth – The Borough

Tell Me My Future, Show Me My Destiny — Aldgate

The Borg Cubes – O2 North Greenwich

The Cloud Minders — Cubitt Town

137

The Dawn Of Man – Canary Wharf

The Doomsday Machine – Cheesegrater Bishopsgate

The Lift – Paddington Basin

The Lines Are Drawn –
New Street Square

Vertigo 'Retro' – Office Life London

Vertigo 'Skyline' – Office Life London City – Cheapside

Vertigo 'The Next Phase' – Office Life London City

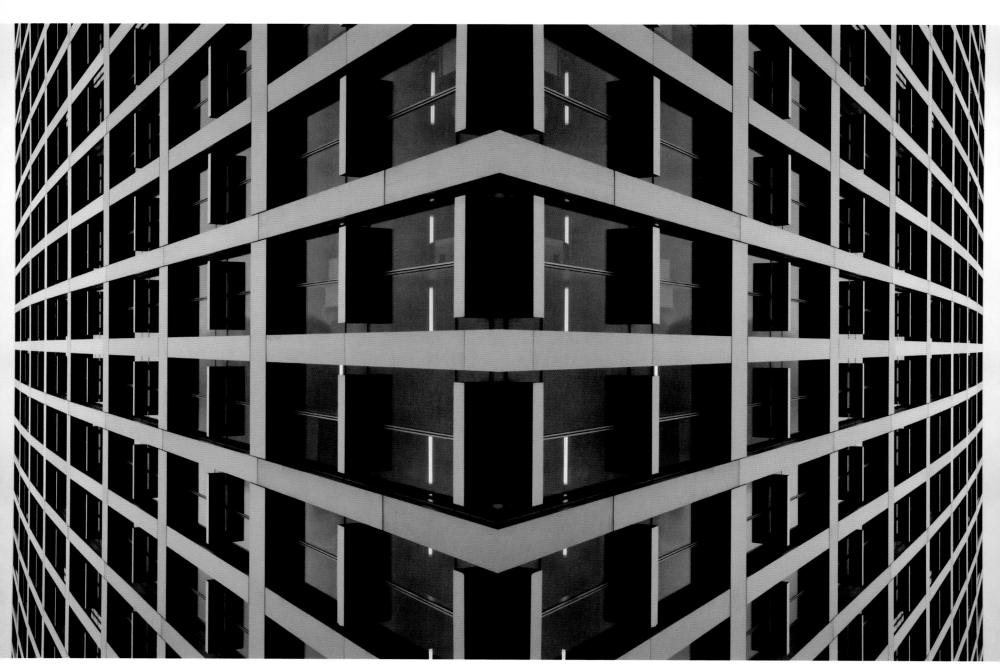

Vertigo 'Visage' — Office Life London City — London Wall

Vultures Circling – London City Life

When Can I Leave – Tower Hill

When Can I Go On Holiday
— Cubitt Town

The Shard A City Reflects

London – Architecture &
Christmas – Southwark

THE WOMEN OF WORLD WAR II

*The National Monument to the
Women of Worls War II*

London Central Mosque aka
Regent's Park Mosque

Duck Heaven — Welcome To Chinatown Resturants

Miracles May Happen But Nothing Is Happening Yet –
London Urban City Life – No1 Poultry

Greening The City – Fen Court
Garden & Willis Building

London Eye Blossom Spring

The Dark Crystal – The Shard

London City Life On
The Edge – The Sequel

Millbank Tower Trilogy

Ministry Of Defence Headquarters Whitehall

161

On The Wall – Shoreditch Street Art

*Shape Of The Future – London
City Life (The Shard, The Walkie
Talkie & The Cheesegrater)*

Sunset On Battersea Power Station —
Restoring A London Icon

Tate Modern Gallery – Turbine Hall

165

The Dome St Paul's Cathedral

The World Famous 'Don't Feed' – Chubby Pigeon

All Over Curves — Walkie Talkie

Tower Bridge Night Lights

Driving Under The Thames

*Watching Over Us – Houses of
Parliament & Westminster*

172

Where Eagles Dare – London City Office Life

Another Canary Wharf Entrance

Buckingham Palace At Night – London

Shard Under Construction

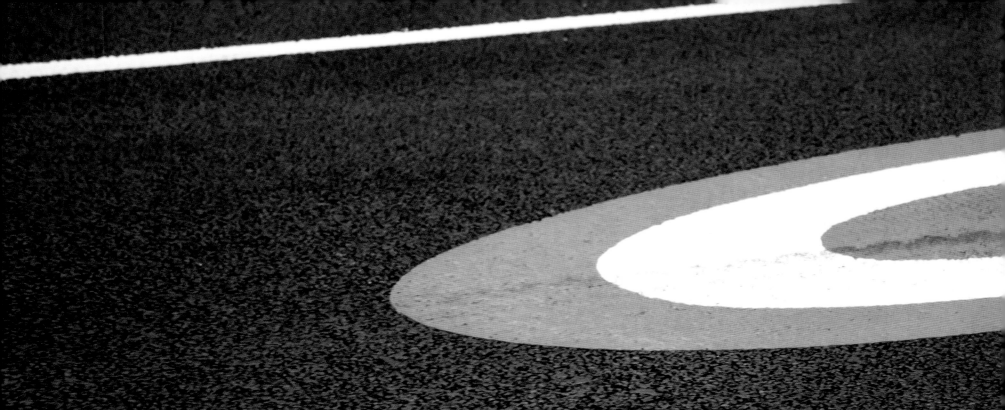

The Congestion Charge

The Monument to the Great Fire

Is Wonderland really a wonder.. –
Canary Wharf Underground

Secret Of My Success - Cheapside

Reflected Wings On A Steel Butterfly — Bankside

Patterns Of Force – Lloyds Building

Another Good Morning London —
City Office Life

Balance Of Terror –
Lloyds & Cheesegrater

So Shines A Good Deed In A Weary World – St Helen's Building

Tears Fall Down Without Me Noticing – Willis Building

The Doctor Is Not In – Closed Off Underground

By Dawn's Early Light

Certainty Is Fleeting

Towards The Tower — London

Tower 42 London City Office Life

Running Out Of Room – Southwark

My Life My Way My Rules –
Bankside

Night Face Off –
Bishopsgate

Office Life Through The Window – Fleet Street

When Dinosaurs Ruled The Earth – Canary Wharf

Before Freedom — Aldgate

Canary Wharf & The Dome

St Pauls Cathedral – Night Lights

You Can't Do This If You Don't Have
A Dream (London Geometry) Bankside

The Space Between – Millwall Dock

Pride – Fleet Place

City Of London Information Centre –
Carter Lane Gardens

The Wind Blows Painting The Atmosphere

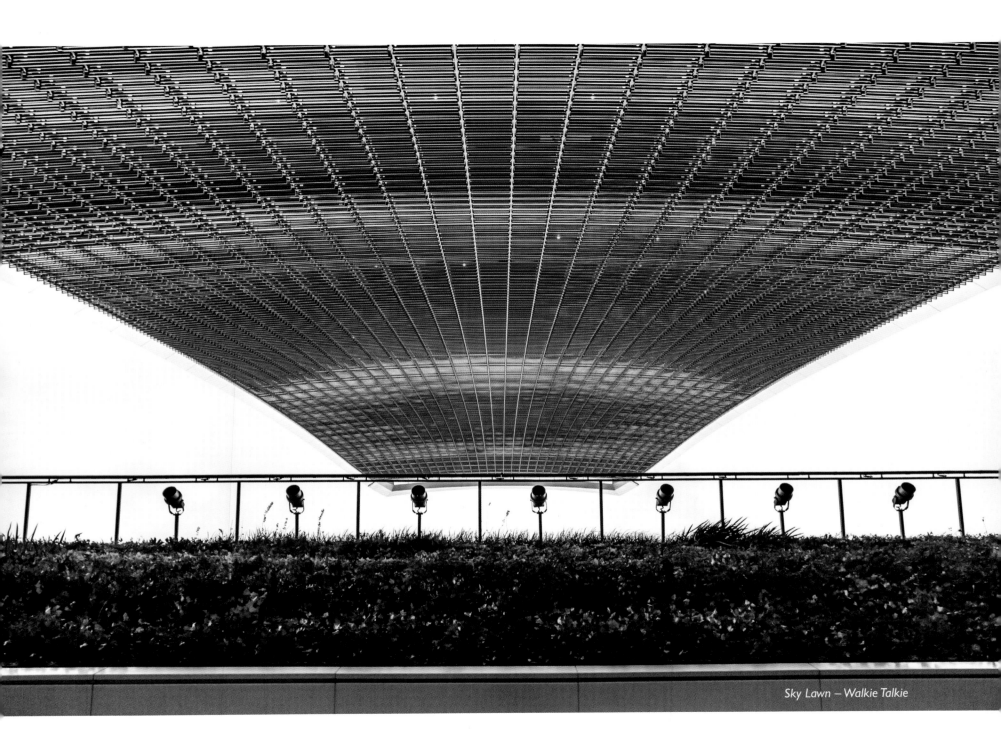

Sky Lawn – Walkie Talkie

The Ghost of Wind — Bankside

From Here To Eternity –
Millennium Bridge

Nelsons Tomb – St Pauls Cathedral

Age Of The Mayans – London City

Dawn Of A New Day In The New World

New Wave – London City Life

I Can't Hold Back — Cubitt Town

Deja Vu – London Office Life

Live Life Like You Stole It – London City

Under The Tower — Nine Elms

219

The wheel only worked for the man pushing it from behind – Canary Wharf

You Know What's Missing – London City Office Life

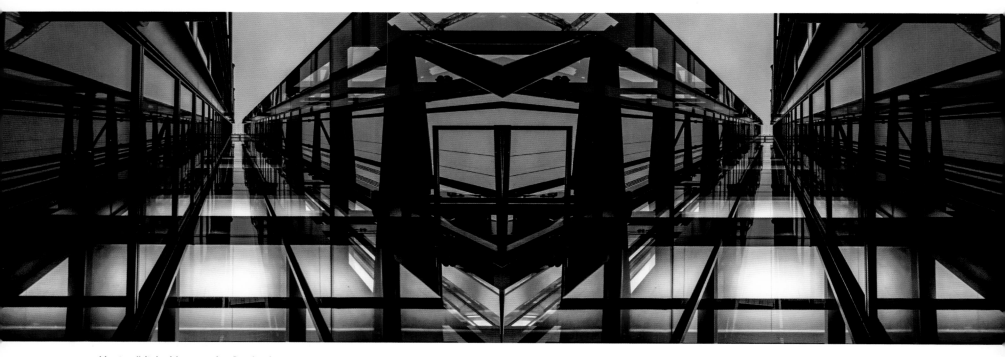

Vertigo 'Night Harmony' – Bankside

Unfathomable is the realm of impossibilities – London City Office Life

Eye Under The Tower – Nine Elms

An Idea Is An Idea Until You Make It Happen
(London City Symmetry)

225

It's All Make Believe — Isn't It

Vertigo 'Lace' – Park House
Oxfrod Street

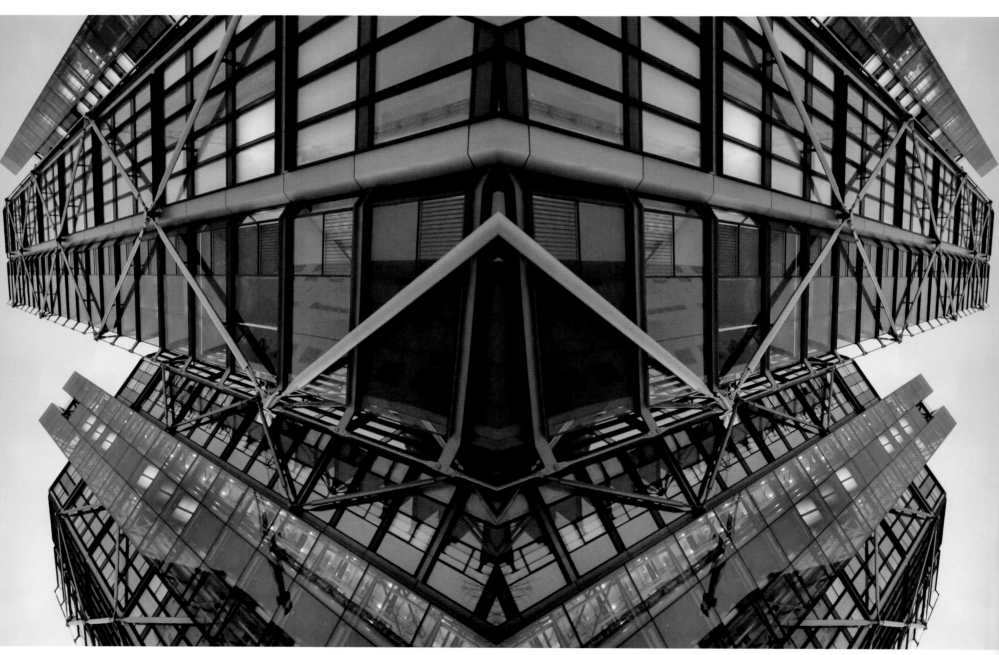

Face Of The City 'Origins' — London

The Face Of The City 'Android' – London

The Face Of The City 'Architect' – London

The Face Of The City 'Centurion' – London

The Face Of The City 'MetalOrganic' – London

The Face Of The City 'Oculus' – London

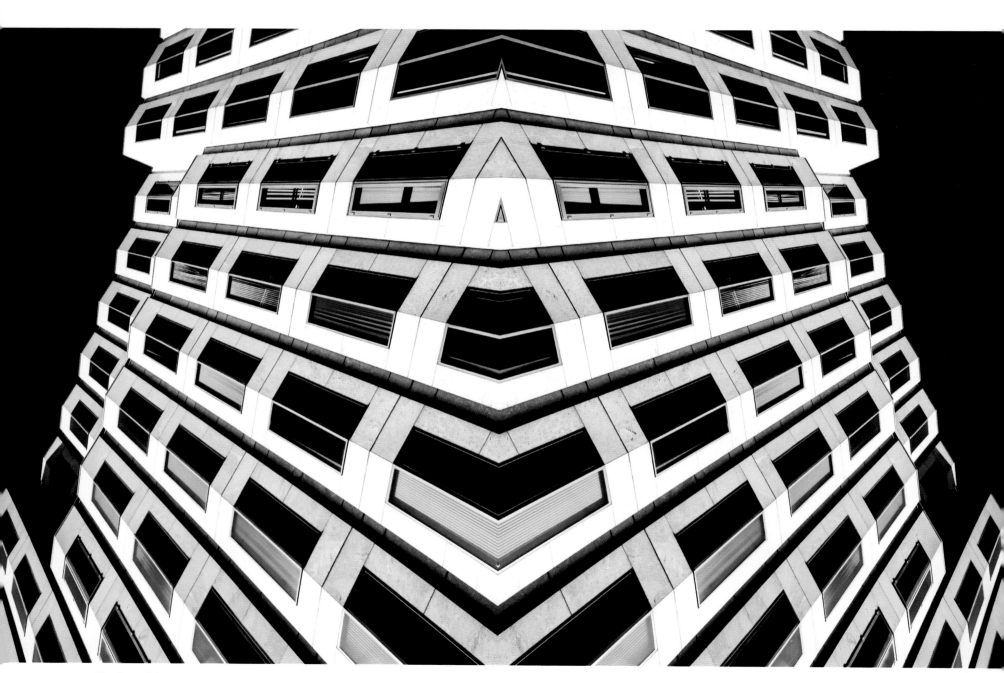

The Face Of The City 'Stormtrooper' – London

The Face Of The City 'Tint' — London

The Face Of The City 'Tron' aka 'Dead Space' – London

The Face Of The City 'Ultron' – London

The Face Of The City 'Vector' – London

The Face Of The City 'Walkie Talkie' – London

First published in 2015 by New Holland Publishers Pty Ltd
London • Sydney • Auckland

The Chandlery Unit 009 50 Westminster Bridge Road London SE1 7QY United Kingdom
1/66 Gibbes Street Chatswood NSW 2067 Australia
5/39 Woodside Ave Northcote, Auckland 0627 New Zealand

www.newhollandpublishers.com

A record of this book is held at the British Library and the National Library of Australia.

ISBN 9781742578040

Managing Director: Fiona Schultz
Publisher: Alan Whiticker
Project Editor: Jessica McNamara
Designer: Peter Guo
Production Director: Olga Dementiev
Printer: Toppan Leefung Printing Limited

10 9 8 7 6 5 4 3 2 1

Keep up with New Holland Publishers on Facebook
www.facebook.com/NewHollandPublishers